GW00402452

Memories of the Brickyard

and other stories

by

Kit Lawie

Marden Hill Press
2007

Published in 2007 by Marden Hill Press
Brickyard House, East Keal
Spilsby, Lincolnshire PE23 4HA.

ISBN 978-0-9538078-4-0

Typeset and printed by Cupit Print
The Ropewalk, 23 Louth Road, Horncastle, Lincolnshire LN9 5ED.

Preface

We came to East Keal in the summer of 1993. One of our first outings in this part of Lincolnshire was to sheepdog trials at Skendleby where we met Kit Lawie and her brother Fred Shaw.

We soon found that they had both been born in our house at the Brickyard and lived there throughout their early years. A few days later we met Kit again at her own home in Toynton All Saints when she began to tell us about some of her memories of living at the Brickyard. This was the beginning of our friendship. We were so lucky to have met Kit on that very special summer's afternoon in August 1993.

For us, these tales told in Kit's own particular way are powerful and enduring reminders of a past that could so easily fade but should not be forgotten. I hope you too will enjoy her memories.

Michael Richardson

Brickyard House
East Keal
Spilsby
Lincolnshire

September 2007

Contents

EAST KEAL, near SPILSBY, Lincolnshire.
To be LET, and entered upon at Martinmas next, or
sooner, if required,

THE old-established BRICK and TILE YARD,
with an excellent arched Kiln, nearly new, a Pug
Mill, and very good and capacious Shades.

Also, a well-built Brick and Tiled Dwelling-house,
with Barns, Stables, and other Out-buildings. The
house contains 2 low rooms (about 20 feet by 18 feet),
6 sleeping rooms, kitchen, dairy, and pantries; adjoining the house is a very good Garden and Orchard,
planted with choice fruit trees, with Garth, Brick-yard,
and Leas, containing 5 Acres (more or less).

Also, a Piece of rich Arable and Pasture Land called
the Hollow Close, containing 5 Acres (more or less).

There is a good bed of excellent Clay, with a suffi-
cient supply of Sand and Water, to carry on the above
business.—Further particulars may be known by apply-
ing to Mr. Rainey, surveyor, or to Mr. Jarvis Rainey,
auctioneer, both of Spilsby.

East Keal, near Spilsby, Sept. 12, 1843.

Memories of the Brickyard

Part One

The 1930's

Though born in East Keal I experienced no feeling of being part of the village in my early childhood. Brickyard farm with Highfield and The Glebe formed a triangle which was the boundary of my parish for the first five years of my life.

The lane still had a grass strip down its centre and high hawthorn hedges sheltered our comings and goings. The early 1930's saw it upgraded and stoned overall, with a lengthsman, Mr Frank Bell, employed to sweep the road and keep the verges tidy. He seemed extremely elderly with very few teeth, but always had time for a chat with me. His lonely occupation was only broken by the passing of the odd bicycle or farm cart and the steam ploughers on High Barns farm which were quite spectacular. We watched for hours. The farmer's two yellow Rolls Royces were rare sights too, open tourers with the well remembered number plates: DO 1 and DO 2.

In the hard times of the early thirties our car, a 'Model T' Ford was laid up. Eventually consigned to the orchard it became our playhouse. At four, I had some early driving lessons from my six year old brother before it rotted away under the walnut tree. A pity we couldn't foresee the coming value of such vintage vehicles. With its wooden spoked wheels, two gears and celluloid side-windows, it was a novel plaything but worth nothing at the time!

King's Stores grocery van delivered on Fridays, with paraffin tin on the running board. I still wonder how Sid Ashton managed to dispense this without tainting the foodstuff. It must have taken some care! Often only the basic tea, sugar and flour were ordered. We had our own bacon, lard, butter, eggs and milk. Mother rarely went shopping.

Father took rabbits to the Monday market auction and operated a trucking deal with Braimes, the fishmonger's stall. This payment in kind worked well enough in deepest winter although harsh words were heard in July at the appearance of a stone of cod whose shelf life, without a fridge, was about four hours. But, even so, a surfeit of fish made a change from rabbit and bacon.

Wine making with cowslips, dandelions and blackberries filled the back dairy. Popping corks and exploding bottles were sounds we were well used to. Elderflower champagne was my tipple as a five year old!

Listening to the wireless
By the mid thirties Grandma Longland had died and Mother inherited her wireless, a temperamental box of tricks that would function only with the weight of a flat-iron on its dial and a matchstick wedged under its volume switch. It was nevertheless a great novelty for Mother and me.

J.B.Priestley had a tea-time "slot". I particularly remember his stories of early cycling days in the Yorkshire Dales and Arthur Marshall's rambling monologues delivered with such gentle humour.

Also very entertaining were talks by Basil Boothroyd of his early experiences as a young Lloyds Bank clerk in Horncastle, particularly his account of a Lancaster's bus ride to Skegness one pre-war Monday. On passing through Spilsby he witnessed a milling group of peasantry gathered round the Franklin statue and wondered was it market day or a street accident? He settled on the latter as the Tetford based bus carried him eastward, concluding that it was a town of bedraggled women and drunken men!

Before the arrival of this wireless the only musical, and I use the term loosely, entertainment I remember was the rare occasion when Mr Billy Ellerby would trudge across the fields of Twentylands from Hundleby in the dark, carrying his old wind-up gramophone and a few very worn records. He'd bring two boys from his large family and Mother would give them supper after crackling performances of "The man that broke the bank in Monte Carlo", "Two Lovely Black Eyes" and "Red Sails in the Sunset" to which we listened with rapt attention before they set off again into the dark on the long journey home.

Aunt May
Father had an unmarried cousin May whom we all thought very old-fashioned and quaint and something in LNER administration, a relatively well-paid job. She

would come for a few days in what we assumed were her oldest clothes, chosen presumably as being quite good enough for a farm stay. I remember particularly an old green felt hat which she left behind for 'the girls'. My sister and I, quite affronted, immediately consigned it to a rummage sale, only to have to recover it at some expense later, for she'd had second thoughts and asked for its return.

On a Sunday evening she would stand in our living room and sing hymns unaccompanied! Florence Foster Jenkins was a nightingale by comparison! I say no more but May thought it her duty to brighten our lives and so she did! Her eccentric ways amused us all.

The cinema comes to East Keal
Two of my brother Fred's friends, Norman and Sidney Desforges, who lived in the cottage opposite the village pump, took over their granny's pigsty to convert it into a cinema. Silent movies of course! Capacity of building two plus operatives: one brother the projectionist, the other the sound man with coconut shells, thunder sheets, bicycle bells, the lot! — a very inventive pair of young boys they were! The admission a halfpenny or two toffees was nevertheless by invitation only! But Fred, having pulled a string or two, got me invited to a Saturday morning performance – the film: King George the Fifth's funeral! – A newsreel, I was impressed!

Norman Desforges

OPENED
1934

Whether it was actually snowing heavily on that sad occasion – or was the technical quality of the output less than perfect? – I gave them the benefit of the doubt since I knew the King did die in mid-winter! But as I trotted home past the Stainton's off-yard, I wondered if this pigsty conversion at the bottom of Alban House garden (the bay-windowed property next to the War Memorial) was a typical example of 'a cinema' I'd heard so much about. I decided one would not be expected to enter a proper cinema on one's hands and knees and there'd surely be something to sit on. But what inventiveness these young brothers showed. Norman was also artistically talented, despite being physically handicapped and never able to attend school. Not that art was in the forefront of a village school's curriculum in those days!

The cinema was closed after an outbreak of chicken pox brought on by a customer named Alf Elley from down Fen Lane. We were ill for weeks. The conditions in the pigsty could not have helped much.

School
I found my first day at school an ordeal. Knowing none of the children at the village school, well outside the boundary of my own parish, the infant teacher had my full attention. Miss Holt (later Mrs Geo. Bradley) was an imposing figure, her thirties dress, the draped collar, the clinging skirt, its filmy loose panels ending in points around her ample calves and patterned in large cabbage roses the colour of butter. Describing the creation to Mother she agreed – Miss Holt was indeed very fashionable.

Living locally, there was very little teachers didn't know of pupils' families, their problems, financial state and intellect, and they made allowances accordingly. Parents and teachers had grown up in the same village, for there was very little movement of families in those days.

Flitting
The only flitting of which I was aware was among some farm workers, living in tied farm cottages, who on April 6th, Lady Day, would have to vacate their homes if the owner didn't re-engage them for a further year. This would then force them to seek work with another farmer who had a cottage available. The removal of chattels, chickens and children by horse and wagon, could sometimes involve a long journey taking most of the day and ending down a long farm track. For the children, there would then be yet another long walk to a new village school.

Good workers and reasonable employers finding themselves well suited didn't need to join this yearly shunt. By the 1940's this system was slowly disappearing.

Sheep dipping
Sheep dipping at the Brickyard for flocks from a wide area, some driven seven or eight miles, took place over a couple of weeks every June. The local policeman turned up on his bike and with watch in hand would check that the statutory two minutes immersions were adhered to.

The most memorable dipping day was June 26th 1936 to be precise. My brother and I were awakened to be told that Grandfather Shaw had died suddenly and quite unexpectedly at The Carrs. Mother had to dash off and said we needn't go to school that day. After getting over the initial shock and sadness, a day off school was a little compensation to us, and on dipping day too! with all its comings and goings. But we were in for an extraordinary experience in our young lives for, about mid-day approaching very low over Old Bolingbroke, we saw a huge Zeppelin, a most menacing sight indeed. We screamed to Father, engrossed in activity at the dip dyke, who, deafened by the din of hundreds of sheep penned around him, failed to hear it until it was right overhead.

In the absence of Mother, we felt most alarmed as this enormous marrow-like object passed slowly over, casting a weird shadow across the house. The words 'Graf Zeppelin' could be clearly seen as were the figures moving about in the gondola-like undercarriage. We ran up to the footpath and watched until it was a mere pin-point over Gibraltar Point.

On a spying mission, so rumour had it, across England, photographing items of interest for the Third Reich! I wonder what they made of this phenomenon of flocks and flocks of sheep converging through a network of lanes to East Keal dipping station.

At seven I wasn't convinced it was of this planet and feared a rope ladder might be lowered and strange creatures issue forth – two such momentous events on the same day! There must be a connection: was this awe-inspiring craft the means of raising Grandfather to heaven?

By evening I'd thought better of posing the question to Mother on her return from The Carrs, weary from all the problems involved in dealing with Grandad's death and funeral arrangements. The appearance of a Zeppelin of little concern to her, we were a little crestfallen! But we made the most of what we'd seen when returning to school at West Keal the following day, for none of the children had been allowed to see it! Oh, what an account we gave!

Ice Skating

After a few hard frosts, the ice on the Brickyard pit would be the gathering point for all the local people. Word would go round "Shaw's pit is thick enough".

Saturday afternoons and Sundays, they would appear up the lane or across "Whopper's" footpath, skaters and onlookers: Saturday mornings were still working days.

Sometimes as many as forty people would be on the ice, from as far afield as Bolingbroke and Dalby. The noise from an impromptu ice hockey match could be heard in the village; this attracted even more onlookers.

These matches had no umpire or time limit. Players simply dropped out from exhaustion, to sit on the pig cratch to remove skates and trudge home in the early dusk. Some stayed on to skate round stable lanterns and, occasionally, a glowing brazier in half an old oil drum.

We seemed to have an inbuilt sense of when not to go on the ice when it could have been dangerous. We'd grown up with it, summer and winter, boating, swimming and skating. In fact, the pond was, I suppose, the boys' chief source of entertainment. Mine was the horses! I spent all my free time with them and their foals.

As a small child I gained an early awareness of class distinction at this pond-side. The local gentry would gather, having presumably contacted each other beforehand, to spend an hour or two skating sedately. They, of course, came during the week when the lower orders were at work – but Fred, as a ten year old and already a very good skater, would join them. They tolerated him. After all it was his pond! I don't ever remember them asking permission to use the ice but nor, I suppose, did the villagers. It was taken for granted and they gave no cause for worry about damage of any sort in those days. 'Light-fingered' people were thinner on the ground, hence the doors of the house were never locked day or night until the 40's and, even then, locking-up simply meant removing the six inch nail serving as a latch on the back door. This was more an indication to callers that one was out rather than to prevent entry!

The outbreak of war brought about the end of winter gatherings on the ice.

Part Two

The War Years

Marden hill, in the north of the parish, was an ideal lookout point for parachutists and invaders. And at critical stages of the war it was manned day and night by army or Home Guard.

With no electricity or mains water at the Brickyard, our wireless, powered by accumulators, was the main source of news. The war was to last for the rest of my childhood.

The first few days

"It'll be all over by Christmas" Granny said as we stood by the pump under the yew tree watching the departure of East Keal Territorials on an open lorry, waving as they left the village. Turning away, she added "but we said that last time"! At eleven, I was her youngest grandchild – she at seventy, widowed and always in black, brimmed hat pulled well down. Her small farm 'The Carrs' was the last property of the parish on its eastern edge.

She'd handed a sprig of 'lads' love' for luck to the young men. I suppose most of them hadn't been more than fifteen miles from home in their lives!

Within days, gangs of men with sledge hammers removed iron railings, scrapheaps, discarded farm machinery and posts for munitions factories.

September 1st, two days before war broke out, saw the arrival of three coachloads of evacuees from the dock area of Grimsby. I remember being in Spilsby with Mother and witnessing the sad sight of children being allocated on the spot by a group of local volunteers and led away with their meagre belongings in brown paper parcels to outlying villages.

Many of the children drifted back home when the expected bombing didn't materialise. A few stayed on, adopted country life and are still with us. We didn't have evacuees billeted with us, much to Mother's relief! But our neighbours the Davisons had two brothers, the McClennans, and the rest of their large family were distributed around East Keal.

Air Raid wardens were appointed ... George Goodman, Joe Middleton, Walter Horton, B. Sharpe and two messengers ... Obadiah Harrison and A Barnsdale.

A first aid post was established in the Manor's garage. Gas masks were carried everywhere. How memorable those school gas attack exercises. My brother often forgot his and was given detention and threatened with an excruciating death.

The removal of signposts, together with a government edict that 'careless talk costs lives' made life interesting! When asked for help by strangers we didn't like the look of, we said "never heard of it" or worse, gave misleading directions! Tradesmen painted over addresses on vans and lorries.

Our bicycling postman, Mr Taylor, was a reliable source of information, news of overnight bombing, plane crashes and other dramas. The bringer of much good and bad news throughout the war. Poor man!

The sky was soon full of loaded bombers – Hampdens at first and later Lancasters circling over Old Bolingbroke and East Keal until all were airborne in formation for raids over Germany. They left at bedtime and returned, the lucky ones, in the early morning. A returning Hampden bomber crash landed within a few hundred yards of the Brickyard early one Sunday morning. Jess and I ran out behind the pit in our night clothes to see that the crew were all safely out, much to our relief. I remember the look of strain on their faces and no wonder, a six or seven hour bombing raid over occupied Rotterdam on that occasion, but night after night somewhere!

The Local Defence Volunteers (known as 'Look, Duck and Vanish) were soon renamed the Home Guard. The firewatchers shared cramped headquarters with them at 'The Laurels' and, as in 'Dad's Army', much was made of this inconvenience! Overnight derisive notes were left for firewatchers as to what to do with cumbersome buckets of sand and stirrup pumps. And there were equally explicit answers regarding Home Guard bayonets. The wit of these missives reached great heights and was the first topic of conversation the following morning among the farm men.

What d'yer mean who goes there?
I'm yer Dad – that's my gun.
And no – you can't have any cartridges.

Open spaces were scattered with farm machinery to prevent planes and gliders landing. Road blocks were in readiness at both ends of the village. Homing pigeons were banned: presumably of use to spies. They were commandeered ... or quickly eaten in many cases. Corn or hay stacks had to be twenty yards apart in case of incendiary bombs.

On hearing church bells

At the outbreak of war church bells were silenced, only to he rung as a symbol of enemy invasion by land or air. Therefore it was with some astonishment to say the least, when in July 1940 we heard the loud ringing of Old Bolingbroke's church bells.

We searched the horizon in all directions. No parachutists. Awaiting the warning peel from other churches in some bewilderment we turned on the wireless where all seemed normal. Within an hour a passing cyclist called over the hedge "Bolingbroke parson's been arrested' before peddling on to spread the news; thus the quiet of that Sunday morning was gradually restored.

Nationally, the event caused quite a stir! and locally rumour was rife: enemy agent, spy, informer? The Rev. Calvin Graham was sent for trial and given two months in Lincoln Gaol for ignoring a Government Order that was, apparently, of some importance. A bit of a rebel!

Our parson, on the other hand, was known for his lack of humour and extreme frugality, only matched by his wife's thrift. Well known was the tale of the remains of a cold bread pudding offered to a poor neighbour for tuppence. No deal was made, for this neighbour and others had already been acquainted with the poor quality of those Rectory puddings. And rumour had it that her chickens had rejected an earlier mildewed offering.

This parsimonious pair were with us for over forty years! He, always a thorn in Granny's flesh. The feeling, I think, was mutual! If subjected to a visit from him in order to continue some argument, she would turn into a raving atheist for weeks. Neither of them had the genius to let sleeping dogs lie.

17

Dunkirk

Pessimists were shunned. We had to keep up our spirits but were all whistling in the dark, especially after Dunkirk when over 337,000 troops were evacuated. East Keal was inundated with Sherwood Foresters, the Duke of Wellington's Regiment and the King's Shropshire Light Infantry. They arrived in Midland Red buses, commandeering every available building and open space: at the Rectory, the Laurels, Windrush and our Manor Farm yard. Cookhouses and nissen huts sprang up overnight. The buses were repainted khaki and hidden under trees; many officers and men were billeted in houses.

The massing of so many army personnel at this high point overlooking the countryside brought home the serious state of the war. We were urged to stay put if the invasion came and not block the roads needed by the army. Florence Brown, aged 88, remembers repairing soldiers' uniforms, torn and blood-stained from Dunkirk beaches while they listened to the news on her radio. Frances Horton remembers Mrs Harry Wright, born to German parents, and her canteen where tea and snacks were served to the soldiers.

Playing in the marl pit on Marden hill my brother and I discovered a hideout dug into the bank and, inside it, a radio transmitter with an aerial hidden in a tree. I was terrified. A spy outfit? Where was he? Lifting the receiver we got an immediate response. Covering our tracks we fled! Hidden, we saw soldiers running up the hill to find it all still intact. Relieved, we returned home. We kept this secret to ourselves for a long time!

On November 10th 1940, Pat Pearson, an evacuee living with the Salters in School Lane, was killed in a road accident near the village pump. His bicycle was in collision with an RAF trailer transporting a huge flashing contraption to a remote fen field: a mobile decoy light used to confuse enemy planes. Pat, by then nearly fifteen, had stayed on after leaving school to work among poultry.

Meanwhile, village life continues

Bone-setter, Harry Clary, plied his skills at Woolham farm. Andrew Thornley brought round milk with yokes, cans and ladle. The Wildman boys baked and delivered bread (and ran many kindly errands). Ida White, teacher, arrived from Willoughby on her motor bike. Arthur Bird came to work at Manor Farm yard on his bike bringing village news.

The Boy Scouts were formed by G.N. Beaulah, head of Beaulah's Canners and Wholesalers, who came to the Laurels in the 1930's. They raised enough money to pay for installing electricity in the school; the lawns of the Laurels were the scene of fetes and dances: and there were whist drives in the school. Thus, social life flourished, making the most of necessity to raise money for the war effort.

On April 12th 1941, in 'War Weapons Week', Spilsby and surrounding villages raised £214,000 from savings. We did have money, for there was little enough in the shops to spend it on.

The soldiers, for their part, boosted trade at the Saracen's Head run by Cecil Howard. His beer quota, delivered on Thursdays, was consumed by Saturday. Precious clothing coupons weren't wasted on underwear – discarded parachute panels in cream silk were fashioned into lingerie.

By August 1941 we took over the land at Manor Farm when the owner, Tommy Worth, a fighter pilot was reported missing over the Channel. Formerly a civil pilot with a Tiger Moth, the plane was kept, wing-tips folded, in a shed opposite Manor Farm. A familiar sight with its wind-sock flying. The landing strip, our 49 acre field, was used also by Jonathan Thornewell of the Laurels, a descendant of Gladstone, four times Prime Minister.

Remarkable for so small a village, with a population of well under 250, to have two civil pilots owning planes when East Keal probably had only four or five cars! Many more horses and carts of course. The 'two acres and a cow' smallholdings were still the norm and many households reared a pig to cure for bacon.

Changes on the land
In spells of warm weather the grass fields of Manor Farm produced large quantities of mushrooms. The shepherd's wife, olive skinned Nellie Stainton, a painfully thin figure in black would be out before daybreak, darting to and fro until with baskets brimming she would set off home, always at a trot. As a small child I imagined mushrooms disappeared with the dew. Why, otherwise, was it necessary to rise so early! We ate them in vast quantities, making ketchup with the surplus for winter soups.

When war came the pastures were all ploughed up and so disappeared the mushrooms for ever I suppose – but not the early rising! Getting up early was never one of my qualities. Father would hammer on the stairs and rant that the day was half over: this could be any time from 6am onwards! However we did scuttle down on his first call once in 1941, hearing "Come on you lot: Hess is here!" Wide-eyed we flew downstairs expecting to see Hitler's private secretary in the yard. Apparently the early news had reported his arrival by plane on the Duke of Argyll's estate in Scotland. Had we expected to see him impaled on father's pitchfork? Feeling cheated I threatened to go back to bed.

In peacetime or war, there existed a certain code of conduct among farmers regarding the borrowing and lending of implements and of labour which worked reasonably well. But I recall one farmer's son arriving horse in hand. "I've come for the hay rake!" he demanded, to be told we were using it ourselves. He persisted and Mother found herself making excuses as to why we should have a slight priority that day. On arriving home Dad was not so amused to find this chap refusing to go away. Mother calmed things down, for the poor fellow wasn't very bright and feared returning home empty handed.

I was much more concerned with his poor old black mare who stood with head down, eyes closed and a picture of misery and, I guessed, never having had a kind word or a pat in her life. So I made a fuss of her, thereby seeming, I suppose, to encourage the chap to hang on. A good scolding awaited me when he'd gone. But I'd have hugged the horse of Attila, whatever his errand.

There was one horse even I couldn't succeed in befriending – a fiery little trap pony belonging to Mr Abraham Lusher, the Raithby builder and chimney sweep. The most gentle-mannered of men, who showed deference to all, the bad temper displayed by his pony couldn't have stemmed from any ill treatment by him. When his day's work with us was over this defiant creature would take the gateway at full gallop and on one wheel, missing the left post by fractions of an inch. Elderly Mr Lusher hung on to keep the trap upright. Reins had no effect on this wildly reckless journey back to his Raithhy stable. We watched the sport of his nightly departure with much apprehension.

Despite the war, many events seemed unaffected. Mains electricity had arrived in the centre of the parish by 1941, as had the mains water supply. The local press, though full of photographs of killed and injured servicemen, also carried peaceful countryside reports. Henry Cotton won the Golf Championship at Woodhall Spa. Cricket matches carried on; Skegness Wheelers still cycled through the village at weekends.

But we were quickly shaken from any complacency many times. The frightening glow that filled the north sky on two consecutive nights in May 1942 proved to he Hull burning. The whole waterside area completely enveloped in flames, with 300 killed and 400 badly injured in 24 hours. This put into perspective the handful of occasions that East Keal was bombed and where no houses were hit.

Listed in the 'Lincolnshire Standard', Oct 14th 1944:

High explosive bombs on East Keal in 1941

May 6th	
June 12th	a grass field
August 8th	Fen Lane
August 22nd	Keal Fen

Many incendiaries in 1944:

Feb. 15th	Switchhack: Wheelabout Wood on fire.

By 1942 passenger trains had ceased between Firsby Junction and Spilsby. Only goods trains were running from time to time. Serving village men would get a lift in the guard's van and be seen walking home to Keal.

After June 1942 private cars got no petrol ration and were laid up for the duration. At the Manor Yard we were particularly aware of the many adventures of Jim Stainton whose home was the shepherd's cottage in the nearby paddock. He served in every theatre of war: Burma, Malaya, North Africa, Europe, Norway: an SAS soldier who parachuted behind the enemy lines and was reported missing on more than one occasion. He was much decorated.

Also reported missing in the Far East was Bill Greenwood who had worked at Harry Haw's poultry farm in Church Walk. Later reported a prisoner, he survived the hard years spent in a Japanese camp.

Harry Cheetham and Ron Wright were both injured in Holland and Germany but also recovered.

The sad news of the loss of two servicemen: first on November 28th 1942 Harry Bending, at 26 a rear gunner in a Whitley bomber; he made his home in 'Woodlands', the Miss Browns' boarding house. Formerly a Pearl Insurance agent, I remember him, a large jolly man who rode a motor bike. Then, in 1943 WH (Bill) Tayles, whose home was the Manor gardener's cottage, was also killed. Two grave-faced army officers enquired of us the way across our paddock to break what we feared was the bad news that his parents must daily have dreaded. Mother quoted Wilfred Owen... 'bugles calling for them from sad shires' on hearing the news.

Spring, 1943

One very foggy Sunday morning in the Spring of 1943, my father set out to shepherd the beasts on Manor Farm where he had an interesting encounter. Hurrying, for he had to be on Home Guard training by 10 o'clock, he skirted the Carrs Wood and came upon three figures skulking behind trees. Alarmed by his sudden appearance through the gloom to challenge them to "come on out", suspecting they were enemy airmen, for they wore full flying gear, he was surprised by their enquiry "Where are we?" After a lengthy explanation they convinced him they were on our side and he invited them back to breakfast. I imagine they were torn between mistrust and pangs of hunger, for Dad had the air of an eccentric, well fed tramp who might well have spent the previous night sleeping in a hedge bottom as they certainly had!

Hunger won them over and they followed him home to the Brickyard, relieved no doubt to see a farmhouse materialise through the fog and not a roasting hedgehog impaled on a stick across an open fire and tea stewing in a rusty old tin! which they may well have feared – such was Dad's mode of dress.

Meantime Fred was donning his Home Guard overcoat for his training session, when Dad opened the back door, quite fussy with his three breakfast guests who, alas, were so taken aback by Fred's uniform. For hadn't they spent the last 24 hours trying to avoid this on an exercise of evading capture while trying to get back to base.

Had this wily old devil lured them into a trap and maybe a bit of glory to boast about at morning parade? Ah well, too late, and the aroma of home made bacon and eggs sizzling over the grate won them over, plus Mother's reassurances.

Replenished, warmed and redirected, they were sent on their way in the fog, but not before we learned that the most senior among them was Squadron Leader Guy Gibson! a name we were to hear a short time later, when this man's name and his squadron's were on everyone's lips and a legend still: The Dambusters.

We were glad we hadn't run them in. Sadly, he was killed a year later after flying 173 sorties and within months of the war ending.

I think Lincolnshire claimed 'The Dambusters' as their own; we certainly did.

The Bark brothers, our neighbours at Glebe Farm, were summoned to court for non attendance on Home Guard parade, fined £4 each, equivalent then of two weeks wages. (The Standard, Sept. l8th 1943)

Soon after this more regard was given to vital farm work. Cows had to be milked, hay made and harvest gathered. Twelve hour working days in summer were quite the norm. Tight controls on every aspect of food production were imposed. Much the funniest was 'How to make a proper midden' which rated a mention in the 'Horncastle News' of Nov 18th 1944. Whitehall was invited to come and see the dunghill for themselves!

A shortage of coal meant that by March 1944 men were being drafted into the coal mines. Norman Hodgson, son of the Post Office shopkeeper, had the misfortune to be one of those who had to spend a year below ground.

A Case of Mistaken Identity
My experience of being accused of law breaking is extremely limited but I do recall in the war years one occasion on which our local bobby, a man of few words, confronted me.

Wright's buses plied between the market towns of mid-Lincolnshire and their service to Boston was my only means of escape from a lonely farm life, if only for a few hours. I would dash down the lane on my bike the mile to catch the 2pm red and cream wartime utility bus, its slatted wooden seats, polished only by passengers' bottoms, proved the main hazard. One had to hold tight to avoid sliding sideways and dropping into the aisle; one calculated the risk of this indignity according to which driver was in charge. But it was well worth it for a look at the sparsely stocked shops and then the pictures: 'Mrs Miniver', 'The Way to the Stars', 'Dangerous Moonlight' and anything in which the dishy Leslie Howard appeared!

After one such outing, I was returning with seven rolls of wallpaper, a very scarce item in the war years. I always left my bicycle on the East Keal Post Office railings – one could safely do that in the 40's! – I once left it there for a whole weekend! I got off the dimly lit, unheated bus into pitch blackness, after standing a moment to accustom myself to the dark night, I crossed the road and felt my way along the railings – bicycle handlebars at last!

I set about tying my cumbersome wallpaper on the front, a tedious and lengthy task in the dark, single rolls seemed intent on escaping from the end of this unwieldy parcel. My coat belt was finally brought into service to bind it along the handlebars.

Deciding not to attempt to ride with this ungainly load, I set off. I had no lights but that was nothing new! After a couple of steps, I sensed rather than saw a large figure in my path, my front wheel gripped between the knees of our local bobby! Putting his belt light on he said "Wot do you think you're doing gel? You've been fiddling with my bike for a quarter of an hour. Where do you think you're off to?"

Already under some strain I babbled but made little sense. The doubting tone in his occasional "I see" and the light he shone in my eyes were quite unnerving. The fact that he was quite enjoying this little episode in an otherwise very dull evening didn't occur to me until much later!

I flung his bike back onto the railings and went in search of my own. Plodding after me in silence, he allowed me to go through the whole business of untying and retying my by now fiendishly difficult wallpaper burden. If one roll had escaped, I think I would have knocked his helmet off with it, accidentally of course and under cover of darkness! Another quarter of an hour had elapsed.

"Where are your lights?" Oh, he'd noticed had he! With all the tartness I felt, I said "I had no intention of riding it! One is allowed to wheel one's unlit bicycle, is one not?" (I always thought this a silly rule anyway, since one is a much greater target walking and pushing a bike).

At this point our mono-syllabic bobby surprised me by uttering quite a long sentence. "Pity" he said, "I was almost tempted to let you try to get on mine, to find what you thought was yours had sprouted a crossbar while you were in Boston!" I couldn't see his grin but I could hear it. You can, can't you?

Why my usual sense of humour had deserted me I don't know, but infuriated by this time I got onto the damned bike and rode it off into the darkness. Let him summons me! It wouldn't sound well for him in court! Who'd believe his story – "This sixteen year old girl jumped off a bus, in the dark, to steal a policeman's bike she couldn't have known was there. She then M'lord, spent 15 minutes decorating it with wallpaper, which she claimed was hers. She then surreptitiously tried to wheel it away! When apprehended she said she "thought it was hers". She then found another bike in the vicinity and again claiming it was hers, spent some time lashing wallpaper on to it. After admitting she had no lights on it, M'Lord, she rode away.

On reaching home I related this unlikely story to my mother who by that time feared I'd missed the last bus. Much relieved to find I'd only tried to pinch our bobby's bike, laughing, she said "I think you made his day!"

No summons came! But I never liked the wallpaper adorning our living room for the next few years! The pattern of urns always reminded me of policemen's upturned helmets!

How I wish there were village bobbies around now to keep a quiet eye on things. Someone we knew and trusted and who trusted us! Well, some of us.

Confidence rises

Following 'D Day' confidence rose, though scarcities grew. We were urged to gather all the rose hips for making syrup to supplement the diets of children. Basketfuls were dispatched from Spilsby. Rabbits were unrationed and were dished up daily in some form. In November the Home Guard was disbanded but the men were allowed to keep uniforms for land work. The inevitable rabbit pie supper plus a little earthy rural entertainment by members celebrated the occasion!

The Germans did arrive in East Keal by March 1945 but as prisoners to work on the farms. Brought out daily from Moorby P.O.W. camp, some were billeted with us at the Brickyard and others with the Johnsons at the Glebe.

By a strange coincidence, one of the German gunners protecting the Moine Dam on the night of the Dambusters' raid, was one of the prisoners at the Moorby camp who came to live and work with us at the Brickyard. Peter was a quiet village carpenter from Tuttlingen in the Black Forest. He built us a workshop, repaired gates and did jobs in the house. He also made a bacon smoker, the envy of all our neighbours who arrived with flitches and hams for his attention and advice.

Peace
Peter was the first prisoner to be repatriated, on compassionate grounds. His brother had been killed in Russia and his 75 year old mother was trying to keep a small-holding together.

His place was taken by Heinz. He was the camp's interpreter and had been a pilot who survived a mid-air collision with another of his squadron. He spent two and a half days in a dinghy off Ramsgate in January 1943 and was shipped out to Canada for the duration of the war, on the same ship as Churchill but well below decks.

Heinz was the last of the prisoners to leave, during the great snowstorm of April 1947.

**Heinz was one of the prisoners of war who worked on the farm
and was billeted in the living room of our house.**

Part Three

After the War was over

The most striking change over the war years, in the countryside at least, seemed to me to be the disappearance of horses from the farms. In 1939 they were the sole power on the land and on the roads. But by 1946 the tractor was much more in evidence and the remaining ageing horses did only the odd jobs around the yard. By the late 1950's they were all gone. I found this very hard to accept.

Christmas entertainment

The Christmas period involved inviting the Johnsons over from Glebe Farm for an evening meal, a game of cards, a glass of Green's Ginger Wine and a bit of farm gossip. There would be a return visit, for an even more substantial meal and an evening of homely entertainment. Mrs Johnson opened the proceedings with recitations in a broad Lincolnshire dialect. Her first item 'The Inventor's Bed' delivered quite straight-faced and therefore very comical. 'A Piece of Binder Twine' followed, equally well done. We asked for more.

There came a moment when the Shaws were prevailed upon to do something. But we had no talents to speak of and Mother would rescue us by asking their daughter, Betty, to play the piano. She was, and still is, an accomplished pianist and would give us a bit of Chopin, Liszt or Rachmaninov. Their family performance was rounded off with Mr Johnson's rendering of 'To be a Farmer's Boy' executed with more volume than was necessary given the size of the room! But who were we to nit-pick?

Heinz, our German prisoner with us on one occasion, volunteered to sing some lieder on our behalf. Betty accompanied him, saying "Get started! I'll pick it up after a bar or two!"

We finished the evening with Mrs Johnson's delicious toffee, proffered in almost unmanageably sized pieces. Silence descended until we'd regained control, to give our thanks, relight the lantern, pull on our wellies and return on foot. Encountering their massive grey cart horse, Violet, dozing in the shelter of the high hawthorn hedge dividing their land from the Davison's Highfield Farm, I gave her withers a big hug, as usual, before turning in.

Bringing home the bacon – a moving tale
Winter at the Brickyard usually saw the arrival of the steam threshers and the cut-box, an engine-driven contraption for chopping oat sheaves into horse feed, frost proofing the pumps and stocking up on paraffin, candles and firewood. But most important was the killing of the pig for the year's supply of bacon which, with wild rabbits, was our staple meat diet, especially in the war years. Rationing continued until 1953.

The winter of 1947 was the most memorable – the storm didn't start till February 15th Fred's 21st birthday! The drifts so deep, leaving no trace of hedge and lanes, and we were not to get out by road for nearly seven weeks.

The problem of bringing home the slaughtered pig from Manor Farm proved quite an expedition, which fell to me. I set out across the fields to harness Smart, my favourite among the farm horses, and backed her into the float – a large trap used for light jobs ... light jobs! Well it would have been, given reasonable conditions – or a road!

After loading flitches, chines and various bowls of offal, we entered the horse field after digging the gateway clear of snow. Incidentally, this field was used to keep horses during the Civil War. Many horse-shoes from that period have recently been found there. In my memory it was the village football ground, but I digress. Back to the battle of the bacon. Jolting past the goal posts, I turned to see a pancheon full of small intestines, the tharms, swilling from side to side until one end slithered over the edge and snaked its way across the trap floor to disappear through a hole in the boarding. This continued until the pancheon was empty. Not daring to stop for fear of getting stuck, I drove on to the next gate where I tied up a puffng Smart. Realising the importance of (Oh, the things we thought important!) recovering these tharms vital in the making of sausages – I had to retrace our route. Knee deep in snow, I eventually located this slimy intestine and reeled in about 20 yards of it. Returning to the trap I threw the disgusting mess into a bowl of trotters and the pig's head – the raw materials for brawn making.

We set off again over the hill and across the dyalings, Smart's girth-band brushing the snow. She had courage, that horse! and did everything asked of her, and willingly! The hero of this battle! Reaching the chestnut trees that bound the orchard fence I lugged it piece by piece over the fence, past the horse pond and oak tree and on to the salted bench in the back dairy

Retracing our steps was a little easier. After feeding and stabling Smart I walked home to two or three days of sausage making, boiling the lard, brawn, pork pies and distributing pigs' fry to neighbours, all on foot of course.

It was April before we saw the lane cleared of snow. Ironically, we'd had a new Austin 10 delivered two days before the start of the storm but hadn't been able to use it, or even get it out of the garage! Very frustrating. I remember Fred starting it and he and I sat in the closed building and very nearly gassed ourselves with the fumes while day-dreaming about eventual outings.

Attending the livestock and milking the house cow were the only jobs to be done on the farm. The menfolk were free to go snow-digging for the local council.

My brothers and Arthur Bird often recalled their experiences when trying to open up the main road at Winceby in the valley known as 'Slash Holler' — the hollow of Battle of Winceby fame. They hung their jackets over the telegraph poles which just peeped above the depth of snow. At one point they found themselves standing on a shiny green surface and found it was the roof of a double decker bus! Abandoned and empty of corpses they were glad to discover, for it had been there some weeks!

I think Winceby has seen more than one battle!

Potted Partridge
At the top end of the Brickyard garden there were always a couple of chick-rearing huts. Bought in as day-old pullets, they spent the first three months under the pear and codling apple trees. Predators (magpies were a pest), had to be discouraged one way or another from killing chicks or devouring their ration of food.

Particularly irritating were a covey of partridges who appeared at feeding time every morning. So a plan was hatched between Mother and my sister Jess to stop the blighters! Before letting the chicks out, the trough was baited and lined up to the open landing window through which was menacingly poked a twelve bore double barrel.

In they came, through the hedge under the pear tree and lined up greedily at the trough. Jess squeezed the trigger once, the old house vibrated. Then she belted up the brick path to find feathers everywhere. Stunned silence from the hundred chicks in the hut and dead partridge everywhere!

Jess was a good shot – a trough like a colander of course! But game pie for a week!

Through the library window

I'm all for a relaxed atmosphere in a library, but an incident over forty years ago was too much for most of us. It was just before the 50s with its more formal behaviour. I suppose that's why the details of this true story remain so clearly with me.

Clothes coupons and food rationing were still in force, with continuing scarcities in many things, though books were beginning to appear on the shelves. Our little library was housed in a downstairs sitting room of one of a row of terraced villas. One very hot day five or six readers were perusing the meagre selection of books, in complete silence of course, as we were bid. How immaculately we behaved in those days! However, on this occasion we were sorely tried, for at the wide open window appeared the woman who lived next door, a well built blonde in her early thirties. I remembered her being crowned as the Town's Carnival Queen just before the war! As a child of ten I was so puzzled as to why she rode on the back of a Parson's coal lorry!

Back to the window, through which this cheerful blonde displayed a pink brassiere, there followed in a loud stage whisper to the librarian "Would this fit you Angela, I got it in Lincoln. I can't get into it, it's never a 38C, the label must be wrong. What size are you?" This had a disturbing effect on the rest of us. In those days such a garment was not usually shown openly and in a public place in mixed company!

We grabbed the nearest book, pretending to be engrossed; mine was 'Spot Welding' a subject about which I neither knew nor cared. We awaited the librarian's answer. "Is it boned? I always have Gossard's boned." Her laid-back manner implied that this sales approach was nothing out of the ordinary in the day's work. I wondered what other items or services had been peddled through this window, or auctioned off to unsuspecting readers!

We all managed to resist staring at the bosom in question, but were by then experiencing some difficulty with our concentration to say the least! Our Church Warden had his 'Golden Treasury' upside down, my 'Spot Welding' was beginning to quiver, lips were being bitten. At this point the neighbour launched another attack, her ample fists thrust one in each bra cup as if to give more realism to the garment's visual qualities. Our posture went, we staggered, we leaned on shelves and on each other, hid faces behind books; some, I imagined were suppressing urges from weak bladders, but we pulled ourselves together and maintained our silence. Rules were rules! Oh we knew how to behave in those days!

When it was finally agreed the garment wasn't adequate for the librarian either, I began to relax, until I sensed a reader nearby had hastily buttoned her fawn cardigan in an effort to avoid an approach from the determined sales woman! By this time the rest of us were thinking only of escape! The poetry lover, probably fearing an enquiry as to the measurements of his nearest and dearest, was edging to the door, which unfortunately lay next to the window in question. I resolved to follow, though surely I wasn't in danger of being accosted. I was then a small 34C.

Excited by our advance, the buxom blonde leaned further in, her parting shot to the man ahead of me was "Pity your wife's so small – in the upstairs region. I mean" ... she meant me! Really!!

His embarrassment was complete. We gained the outer door, he touched his hat but couldn't bring himself to look at me and turned to go. I was leaning on the doorpost to get a grip on myself when the vicar's wife appeared, a kindly soul, sedate and modest. I nodded but couldn't gather enough composure to warn her of the reception awaiting, for, to my now well practised eye, she was indeed a 38C, "spot on" as they say. I had visions of a makeshift fitting room between the 'Westerns' and the 'Religious Studies' sections. What had I missed! I'm sure a deal was struck before the day was over! An offer to knock a pound off rang in my ears as I made for my bicycle – and the decorum of Waite's wines and provisions shop, with its bentwood chairs and personal service at a whisper.

Conclusion

With all the changes in the village and in farming, my dreams are still of those times in the thirties and forties at the Brickyard: the horses, the attics, the seasons of the year and, especially, of Mother whom I'm sure I failed to appreciate and whom, too late. I wish I had tried to emulate.

Postscript

With her tact, quiet humour and her outward calmness in handling difficult situations when we children were young during the lean years of the 1930's and through the hard years of war, I realize now how devoted Mother was to her family.

Father depended on her a good deal. He was very much hands on with the farm men and a workaholic who had little time for finer details, erratic at times, generous on impulse. Mother dealt with all the farm accounts, the banking and wage paying, the gardening and poultry keeping as well as cooking for the family on an old range in the front room.

In her spare time she would read poetry and biographies and listen to talks and music on our old battery-driven Cossor wireless. I remember she liked the music of Percy Grainger, Bach, Holst and Mendelssohn and Doris Arnold's 'Those You Have Loved' on a Sunday evening. She also enjoyed the talks by people like J. B. Priestley, Harmond Grisewood, John Betjeman, Arthur Marshall, Basil Boothroyd, S. P. B. Mais and the young Alistair Cooke. She rarely missed listening to 'The Brains Trust' with Professor Joad, Commander Campbell, Malcolm Muggeridge and Lady Violet Bonham Carter. A particular pleasure for our family was when mother's cousin, Jack Longland, took over as chairman from Freddie Grisewood in the late 1950's.

I believe the greatest sadness in her life must have been when her beloved younger son, Fred, was struck down with polio at the age of twenty-five, just a week after his wedding. He would never walk again – a tragedy they all bore magnificently.

Kit Lawie's brother, Fred, standing
proudly in his Home Guard uniform

"Look, Duck and Vanish"

East Keal commands an uninterrupted view over the Fens and eastward towards the coast, perched as it is on the south-east corner of the Wolds. Thus Marden hill in the north of the parish was an ideal point to look out for parachutists and invaders. At critical stages it was manned day and night by the army or Home Guard.

In the period between Dunkirk and D Day, the men were also taken down to the coast to patrol on bicycles along the sea bank at Huttoft and Chapel St. Leonards. They were transported by Hudson's meat lorries, which they found a very greasy experience – the carcases giving way each evening to Home Guard transportation – such was the urgency of the time. Smears of blood on their uniforms probably added a bit of realism to their efforts of defending England's shores! Their tasks were both to provide an early warning in case of enemy invasion, and to keep a look-out for spies. This danger did exist, as proved at one point by a man found on Seacroft Golf Course who was radioing details about the 'Royal Arthur' to German ships at sea. As this was the code-name for Butlins, not a massive warship as he presumably thought, it is questionable how useful this smuggled information would be.

One very foggy Sunday morning in the Spring of 1943, my father set out to shepherd the beasts on Manor Farm, where he had an interesting encounter. Hurrying, for he had to be on Home Guard training by 10 o'clock, he skirted the Carrs Wood and came upon three figures skulking behind trees. Suspecting they were enemy airmen, for they wore full flying gear, he challenged them to "Come on out", and was surprised by their enquiry, "Where are we?". After a lengthy explanation they convinced him that they were on our side, and he invited them back to breakfast. I imagine they were torn between mistrust and pangs of hunger, for Dad had the air of an eccentric, well fed tramp who might well have spent the previous evening sleeping in a hedge bottom, as they certainly had. Hunger won them over and they followed him home to the Brickyard. Meantime, my brother Fred was donning his Home Guard overcoat for his training session when Dad opened the back door, quite fussy with his breakfast guests who, alas, were taken aback by Fred's uniform. For hadn't they spent the last 24 hours trying to avoid this on an exercise of evading capture while trying to get back to base?

Replenished, warmed and redirected, they were set on their way in the fog, but not before we learned that the most senior among them was Squadron Leader Guy Gibson!, a name often heard a short time later, when his and the name of the squadron were on everyone's lips and a legend still: The Dambusters.

The Standard, on September 14th 1943 reported that the Bark brothers, our neighbours at Glebe Farm, were summoned to court for non-attendance on Home Guard parade and fined £4 each, equivalent then of two weeks wages.

Whilst carrying out firing practice in the grounds of Wainfleet Hall, a live shell was accidentally discharged from a spigot mortar, narrowly missing the army cookhouse nearby. This caused much consternation among the occupants, who emerged white-faced and trembling, their preparation of corned-beef hash abandoned to the settling dust.

Following 'D-Day' confidence rose, though scarcities grew... rabbits were unrationed and were dished up daily in some form. In November the Home Guard was disbanded but allowed to keep the uniforms for land work. The inevitable rabbit pie supper plus a little earthy rural entertainment by members celebrated the occasion!

After local disbandment, six Home Guard members were chosen to represent the East Lincolnshire Battalion in a formal stand-down parade in The Mall. Cyril Parker, then of High Barns, West Keal, was one of those chosen. He remembers being taken by army truck to Retford and thence by train to London, a place he had never been to. Here, Home Guard members from all over Britain were mustered for a march-past before the King, Queen and Princesses, followed by an evening's entertainment in the Albert Hall. The compere was Leslie Mitchell, and Vera Lynn and many top stars of the war years appeared before the 5,000 Home Guard members – quite a night by the sound of it!

A letter through the post

Communication in the early 1950's was almost solely by Royal Mail whether for private or business purposes: a letter posted in the evening was invariably delivered early the next morning.

It was thus that, shortly after I had married and moved to Toynton all Saints, I received a letter through the post inviting me to a money-raising event in nearby Skendleby Psalter. It was the sort of "do" which started with a glass of sherry, a buffet supper followed by an evening of bridge or whist. The particular charity to benefit I've long forgotten but the events of that evening are still with me.

Four fellow guests from my neighbouring village arranged to give me a lift for the five mile journey. I'd planned to meet them at our church gate, living as I do, down a steep farm track and over two cattle grids. Quite used to this ten minute walk in the dark, I knew every stick and stone. A frosty night, my wellies slipped about on the icy track, I'd stuffed a dainty shoe into each of my coat pockets and I set off clutching my contribution to the evening's raffle, a large shiny chrome biscuit barrel – an unwelcome wedding present which I suspected had already done the rounds of other raffles, but I'd filled it with custard creams in the hope of improving its appeal.

My timing seemed spot on, for arriving at the church corner a car sped up and screeched to a halt before me. Was this aggressive driving a hint that we were running late? Opening the rear door I quickly scrambled in, chatting cheerily to its dark interior only to be met with a stony silence. The opposite rear door opened to let out a shadowy figure who, without a word, disappeared into the darkness.

Had there been a row? So unlike these four friends! My chatter dried instantly. After what seemed an age, the driver turned to show the silhouette of a face I didn't recognise and in a broad Lincolnshire accent addressed me "I don't know who the hell you are but 'op it and take your bucket with you". With that the remaining occupant of the rear seat put out a large hand, or was it a foot and propelled me sharply off the seat and out of the car. Smarting at this indignity, bucket indeed! – what quite unnecessary rudeness! The lid had come off the barrel and had skidded away into the darkness as the car sped away. I scrabbled about the icy surface, arms outstretched to locate it. Within minutes my seemingly strange behaviour was illuminated by more headlights slowing down. More cautious now at approaching this car, I awaited some sign from within which was soon forthcoming. Breathless and dishevelled, I fell into the rear seat with some relief and we drove off. I'd planned to slip out of my wellies only to find one shoe missing. The prospect of spending the evening in an elegant drawing room paddling about in my husband's wellie socks five sizes too big for me was not nice, nor was the hilarity shown by my friends when told of the episode with the other car, the details of which they relayed to all the other guests during the evening. My concentration on the game of cards was less than perfect, to say the least.

But then came the raffle! The first prize, a brace of pheasants, was won by one of the couples I'd gone with. Townies originally, they were appalled at the prospect of dealing with dressing the birds and so I promised to pluck and draw them – and then my ticket came out of the hat. Lucky at last I paddled penguin-like across the blue Wilton carpet to be presented with a prize from our charming hostess, "Oh well done, now there's a lovely biscuit barrel or 1 cwt of coal – I expect you'd prefer the biscuit barrel?". I blurted out "no really, I'd rather have the coal, so useful" – (coal was still in short supply in 1950). Only then did it occur to me what a cumbersome, dusty, heavy object it would prove. To impose it on my friends' immaculate car boot was thoughtless., But no – didn't they have a good laugh at my expense earlier? Serve them right! Donning my wellies again, we heaved the eight stone sack of coal – (as they were in 1950) into the boot which had the effect of causing the headlights to illuminate only the tree tops.

The journey home was devoted entirely to how to cope with the burden in the boot. We decided to leave it in the churchyard until morning. By now bright moonlight with hoar frost glistening, we dragged the heavy sack from the boot as the church clock struck midnight. We giggled at our clumsy efforts to negotiate the gate, we rolled the sack behind a gravestone and, puffing and panting, we said goodnight.

I slung the brace of pheasants over my shoulder and headed homeward, quite oblivious of the fact that our activities in the moonlit churchyard were witnessed by an elderly couple from the window of their bungalow opposite, so disturbed by the seemingly macabre scene they spent a sleepless night before ringing the local policeman and, of course, police in the 1950's came when sent for!

And so returning for my prize in the morning I was surprised to find PC Hurst-Carrott prodding at the hoar-covered bundle with his boot. He'd cycled from the adjoining village to investigate as he said "strange goings on at midnight among the grave stones."

I explained the presence of the sack of coal which he listened to without comment. His mind seemed to be on other things. "You don't know anything about a strange woman who tries to get in cars when they pull up, do you?" My eyes widened. "Really!", I said. He collected his bike from the church wall. "Some say she does a bit of poaching as well. She was seen later carrying pheasants, but what she uses the bucket for I can't imagine, can you?" He gave me a long mischievous look before peddling off. I was tempted to ask what sort of man would throw from his car a poor woman whose sole possession would seem to be a bucket!

I enjoyed the thought of this man's wife finding my size 5 party shoe on his back seat and demanding an explanation! Would she have believed his story of a maniac woman with a bucket accosting him?

Of course, my thanks for a most entertaining evening were sent to my host that day in a letter through the post.

And so I close this tale for you:

> To the last detail it is true
> T'was almost sixty years ago
> My eyes not what they were and though
> I'm slower now but on the whole
> I still play bridge – I burned the coal
> My biscuits eaten from the packet
> Still poach a bit – still have the jacket!

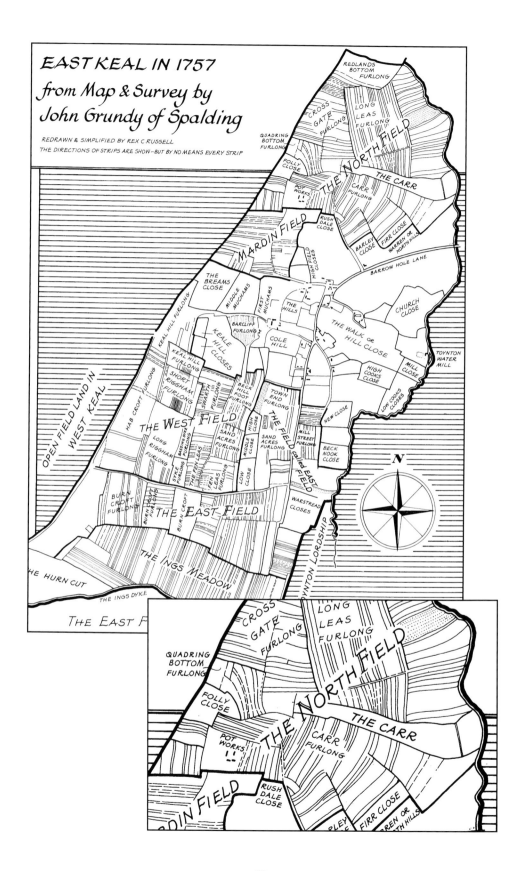

EAST KEAL IN 1757

from Map & Survey by
John Grundy of Spalding

REDRAWN & SIMPLIFIED BY REX C RUSSELL
THE DIRECTIONS OF STRIPS ARE SHOW—BUT BY NO MEANS EVERY STRIP

REDLANDS BOTTOM FURLONG

CROSS GATE FURLONG

LONG LEAS FURLONG

THE NORTH FIELD

THE CARR

QUADRING BOTTOM FURLONG

FOLLY CLOSE

POT WORKS

CARR FURLONG

MARDIN FIELD

RUSH DALE CLOSE

BARLEY CLOSE

FIRR CLOSE

WARREN OR NORTH HILLS

HIGH FIELD CLOSES

BARROW HOLE LANE

THE BREAMS CLOSE

MIDDLE MUCHAMS

FIRST MUCHAMS

THE HILLS

CHURCH CLOSE

KEAL HILL FURLONGS

BARCLIFF FURLONG

KEALE HILL CLOSES

COLE HILL

THE WALK OR HILL CLOSE

KEAL HILL FURLONG

SHORT RIGGHAM FURLONG

SWARTH FURLONG

BECK HILL FOOT FURLONG

TOWN END FURLONG

HIGH COOKS CLOSE

MILL CLOSE

TOYNTON WATER MILL

HAB CROFT FURLONG

THE WEST FIELD

SAND ACRES

HIGH FURLONG

THE FIELD called EAST FIELD

LOW COOKS CLOSES

OPEN FIELD LAND IN WEST KEAL

LONG RIGGHAM FURLONG

BASTNASBYKE FURLONGS

MIDDLE FURLONG

SAND ACRES FURLONG

NEW CLOSE

N

SYKES FURLONG

THE FEN LEAS

LEN LEAS FURLONG

LOW CLOSE

MILL STREET FURLONG

BECK NOOK CLOSE

BURN CROFT FURLONGS

BURN CROFT FURLONG

BURN CROFT

THE EAST FIELD

WARSTEAD CLOSES

TOYNTON LORDSHIP

THE EAST FIELD

THE HURN CUT

THE INGS MEADOW

THE INGS DYKE

THE EAST F...

CROSS GATE FURLONG

LONG LEAS FURLONG

THE NORTH FIELD

QUADRING BOTTOM FURLONG

FOLLY CLOSE

POT WORKS

THE NORTH FIELD

THE CARR

CARR FURLONG

...DIN FIELD

RUSH DALE CLOSE

...RLEY ...

FIRR CLOSE

...RREN OR ...TH HILLS

40

Pots and Pug Mills
by Kit Lawie and Michael Richardson

History

Clearly an early site of pot making, as a John Grundy map of 1757 shows.

Mr Hastings' held the living as Rector of East Keal from 1760 to 1784. He also owned the Pot Works. These were in production on the northern slopes of Marden hill well before the land enclosures of 1774.

Mr Hastings took out a mortgage of £250 on the Pot Works property and then sold it towards the end of the 18th century to a Mr John Goodwin who developed a brick and tile works on the site. Mr Goodwin also built Brickyard House on the adjoining land using bricks made with the local clay.

Notices in the Lincoln, Rutland and Stamford Mercury confirm that there were both a house and a brickyard at East Keal by the beginning of the 19th century. Other owners of the brickyard as well as an earlier potter can also be traced from early issues of the Lincoln, Rutland and Stamford Mercury:

May 30th 1803	Mrs Goodwin, Business of Potter, Brick and Tilemaker died in 1811
Feb. 26th 1813	John Parker, Potter of coarse pots
Oct. 13th 1826	Thomas Smith, died in Horncastle at the age of 80, (formerly a potter at East Keal)
Sept. 12th 1843	advertisement to let by the widow of John Parker (sold to John Dawson of Burgh le Marsh and remained with his family until the 1920s).

Brick making ended at East Keal soon after 1900.

An early mortgagee and eighteenth century patron of Mr Hastings was Charles Brackenbury Carr, a man of many properties including the Carrs Wood and other land in the north of the parish. The Brackenbury Carrs were a notable family in the Spilsby area and one supposes that the name Carrs Wood and the nearby The Carrs farmstead at the north-eastern edge of the parish on the main road to Spilsby, stemmed from this family.

The population of East Keal in the early 1800's was around 450. Comparing this with the 270 of the 1940's means that some very large families were reared in the little mud and stud tiny-windowed cottages that have disappeared in the last two hundred years. The church burial records of those times make very sad reading: twice as many infants and young children died as those of a mature age.

Working at the Brickyard

In conversation with Fred Shaw during the 1950's, the late Mr Jack Johnson of Toynton All Saints recalled working at the brickworks as a boy of twelve in 1898. His working day involved rising at five to walk the two and a half miles through a bridleway via Toynton Watermill, past East Keal church and continuing along the path to Manor corner and the rutted lane of Hoe hill, to arrive at the brickyard by six o'clock for a twelve hour working day. For half the year this would mean a trudge in darkness at both ends of the day! His daily wage for carrying an average of three thousand bricks each day was one shilling and threepence.

The journey by footpath was not, however, a lonely one, for such byways were often the only routes available for farm labourers, artisans, travelling tradesmen, daily domestic workers, schoolchildren and postmen, not to mention the Sunday church – going and courting.

This constant daily grind six days a week for a boy of twelve must, one hopes, have had some lighter moments. One wonders if, in an idle minute, this lad given a surplus scrap of clay, fashioned, moulded and baked the two small heads which survive along with a wall vase and an extremely heavy potty proudly initialled by its creator.

Stories survive also of the bit of poaching that occurred en route: the odd rabbit snare set on the way home and removed the following morning before anyone else was afoot! thus providing a bit of extra protein for men who did such heavy physical work. With their large families, it helped to keep them fit and in a job. For there was naught but charity to fall back on if unemployed!

Brick making

The season of brick and tile making began each October. After removal of topsoil the clay was dug from the northern slopes of Marden hill. It was stacked in large heaps exposing it to the winter frosts and rain, a laborious business, the steel-tipped wooden spade having frequently to be dipped in water to prevent sticking. The heaps had to be turned over at least twice in the cold months to allow the weather to break it down. The men were paid nine pence a ton for this work. A little railway ran from the source of the clay to the pug mill.

By 1811 a new pug mill had been installed. This replaced an earlier one on another site nearby although, in the yard's earliest days of pot-making, the clay would have been kneaded by hand and barefoot. Pot and tile making required a much finer consistency of clay than was necessary for bricks.

The arrival of the pug mill must have greatly eased the preparation of the clay. A horse harnessed to a beam was connected to the centre shaft of the mill which in turn drove the churning paddles. All day this poor animal had to walk in an endless circle round the mill, thus crushing the clay until it was sufficiently malleable and called 'slop'.

Boys wheeled the slops to a bench where men tossed handfuls into wetted wooden bottomless moulds. After packing them down tightly they were cut with a cheesewire and turned out onto a flat-sided brick barrow to be taken to the drying shed (the shades). Before being refilled the moulds had to be redipped in water. In the 1890's a rate of six shillings per thousand bricks was paid to skilled men. Drying took three to six weeks, depending on the weather and a drainage channel carried the resulting water to the laneside ditch.

Great experience and skill was needed in the stacking of bricks in the kiln which took three days to complete. Accurate spacing was vital for the even circulation of heat during firing.

If care was needed in stacking, the actual firing was crucial. Certain dismissal awaited a mishandling at that stage! Planks were placed over the open topped kiln to conserve the heat. Nearly 30,000 bricks could be accommodated in the sixteen-holed kiln which took ten days to fire. Overnight attendance was essential. Fires had to be stoked every twenty minutes to maintain an even heat. An experienced firer would earn three shillings and sixpence a night. A whole month's work could be ruined by a fluctuating temperature in the kiln — a great responsibility!

After firing, the cooling process took a further five to seven days, an anxious time for those responsible. Their first glimpse into the still hot kiln must have brought relief on seeing all was well.

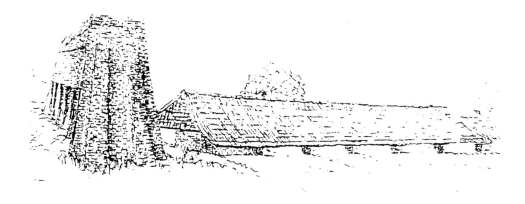

Trees in the vicinity of the brickworks were badly affected by emissions from the kiln. Pollution was rife and many of the potters are known to have died young, victims of poisoning by the lead which was often used for glazing pots. It was not a healthy occupation!

Stories also remain of seemingly well-cooled bricks that set many a wooden cart alight on its way home, much to the consternation, in one instance, of the horse that set off at a gallop, thus fanning the flames heralding its approach to the village and a source of water to douse the fire!

In 1866 Edward Cheffings of East Keal carried on a business of carter of bricks, pots, tiles and sand. One imagines an economic two-way load, carting sand to the pot works where it was much used in the process of moulding and stacking, and carting bricks on the return journey.

The village sand pit was in use until the 1940's before being swallowed up in the widening of the A16 near The Carrs. The sand would also be brought into use for filling the ruts in the Brickyard lane which was, incidentally, called Pot Kiln road in the 18th century and probably much earlier than that.

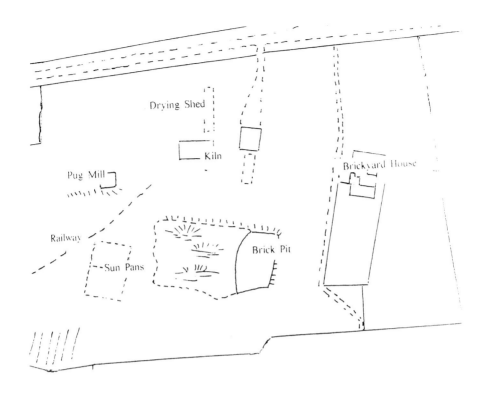

Drying Shed

Kiln

Pug Mill

Railway

Sun Pans

Brick Pit

Brickyard House

Reflections

The brickyard finally ceased production in 1906/7. Only the shades remain, the open sides bricked up and used as a farm shed. The sites of the two pug mills are still detectable as are the distinct signs of the large kiln, the route of the little railway and the nearby sun pans.

By 1921 the land at the Brickyard was being farmed by the Shaw family. It reverted to pasture and during the late 1920's the kiln was dismantled. The bricks were given to anyone able to collect them and horses and carts led away huge quantities. Over the following weeks a smallholder from Toynton St Peter, Stan Johnson, overloaded his cart causing the wheels to fall off, disgorging bricks in the grassy lane there to remain for many weeks. The brickyard remained the Shaws' property until it was sold in 1963.

Unlike other village craft industries, East Keal's brickyard was probably the only source of the village's building materials for over a hundred years and of its domestic pots for much longer. It existed only because suitable clay was available on the spot. And even after the brickyard closed it was still a place where high hawthorn hedges bordered the narrow track and spinneys, and primroses and violets lined the hedgerows providing shade in summer and shelter in winter.

The brickpit is now a pond with yellow iris and lilies; cows and calves swish flies and paddle in the heat of summer, its clay bed dragging at their feet. The brickyard house is still unspoiled, looking out on open farmland.

Kit Lawie with her youngest grandchildren in 2006.

Kit's brother Fred Shaw, with one of his grandchildren in 1994.

Illustrations

Most of the illustrations, including the Brickyard on the front and back covers, are by Kit Lawie. Illustrations by others are listed below:

p. 9	East Keal cinema	Norman Desforges
11	Sheep dipping day	Fred Shaw
17	Our parson	Fred Shaw
40	East Keal in 1757	Rex C Russell
44	Pug mill	J.C.Pyne, 'The Costume of Great Britain' 1808.
52	early pot works at the brickyard	Rex C Russell
inside back cover	pre enclosure fields	Rex C Russell

Acknowledgements

Memories of the Brickyard (1995)
With thanks to my brother, Fred Shaw, for jogging my memory on dates and details. I am also grateful to Norman Desforges for the following note from him to Fred about East Keal's cinema.

This is as I remember the old Pig Sty we made into a cinema at the back of Alban House in the 1930's. We obtained an old "Bingascope" machine, and used to buy offcuts from long films so we only got bits of the story. One we named "Galloping Horses". It was a cut from a Western of the 1920's so we never found out what it was all about. We, that is my brother Sidney and myself, used to charge one cigarette card for the front seats (an old soap box), or two cigarette cards for the back seats (a soap box with a cushion on it). 4 seats in all.
We closed the cinema after an outbreak of Chicken Pox brought on by a customer named Alf Elley from down Fen Lane. We were ill for weeks. The conditions in the Pig Sty could not have helped much.

The information (p.15) regarding dates of the loss of the two servicemen was taken from the East Keal village war memorial. Newspaper references are from the Lincolnshire Standard (Spilsby, Alford and Mablethorpe editions) held at Mablethorpe library.

"Look, Duck and Vanish" (1994)
This was the winning entry in the 1995 'Villages at War' competition organised by 'Heritage Lincolnshire' and supported by the Rural Lincolnshire Community Projects Fund.

A Letter through the Post (2007)

This was a 'commended' entry in the 'Age Concerns in Lincolnshire' essay competition in 2007.

Pots and Pug Mills (1996)

This was the winning entry in the 'Heritage Lincolnshire' 1996 competition on local crafts and skills.

Other suggested reading

Peter C.D. Brears   English Country Pottery, David and Charles 1971.

C.E. Hall (ed)   Look, Duck and Vanish: The Home Guard in Rural Lincolnshire, Heritage Lincolnshire 1996.

Kit Lawie and Michael Richardson (ed)
East Keal: the Story of a Village, Marden Hill Press 2000.

Lincolnshire Branch of the Betjeman Society
Betjeman's Lincolnshire, Marden Hill Press 2006.

Eleanor and Rex C. Russell
Old and New Landscapes in the Horncastle Area, Lincolnshire County Council 1985.

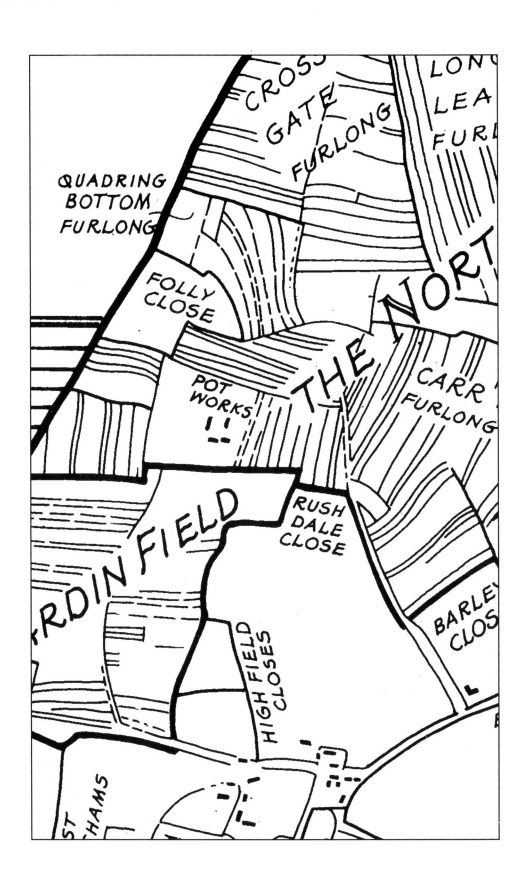